M000232218

"In *101 Simple Lessons for Life*, Marsha Marks shows us how to take faith seriously and life with a sense of humor. This is a poignant, insightful, and often hilarious book."
— LAURIE BETH JONES, author of *Jesus CEO*
and *Teach Your Team to Fish*

"*101 Simple Lessons for Life* is a wonderful mix of the serious and the lighthearted. This is a jewel of a book!"
— FRANCINE RIVERS, author of numerous books
including *Redeeming Love*

"*101 Simple Lessons for Life* is filled to overflowing with humor and spiritual wisdom. Every page is like an intimate visit with a trusted friend who almost always makes you laugh."
— CLAIRE CLONINGER, songwriter, speaker, and author
of *When the Glass Slipper Doesn't Fit* and the E-mail
from God series

"I love to laugh unexpectedly, and that's what I did many times throughout this little volume. But what strikes me most about *101 Simple Lessons for Life* is that the truth in this book is old, and so is the wisdom, but because they come through one person's experience and words, they are fresh and alive and recognizable. We live this stuff every day but may be utterly unaware."
— TRACY GROOT, author of *The Brother's Keeper*

101 Simple Lessons for Life

101 SIMPLE

LESSONS

FOR LIFE

MARSHA MARKS

WATERBROOK
PRESS

101 SIMPLE LESSONS FOR LIFE
PUBLISHED BY WATERBROOK PRESS
2375 Telstar Drive, Suite 160
Colorado Springs, Colorado 80920
A division of Random House, Inc.

ISBN 1-57856-697-5

Published in association with Yates & Yates, LLP, Literary Agent, Orange, California.

Printed in the United States of America

This book is dedicated to my five-year-old daughter,
Amanda Joy Marks.

When she was little I sang her this song,
and when she is older I will give her this book—
and still sing her this song:

"I got a girl name a Mandy Mew,
She's so sweet I don't know what to do.
I love her, oh yes, it's true.
I got a girl name a Mandy Mew."

Special thanks to my editor,
Elisa Fryling Stanford,
who came into my life as a gift from God
and remains in my life as a reminder of his wonder.

Contents

Introduction 1

1. Actions and What Follow Them 3

2. Adoration 4

3. The Availability of God 5

4. Being Born Again 6

5. Belief 9

6. Best Friends 10

7. Bitter into Sweet 11

8. Blessing Us 14

9. Boldness 16

10. Bragging 17

11. The Child Who Had No Manners
    (and She Was Dirty, Too) 18

12. Choices 21

13. The View of the Common Man 22

14. Communication 23

15. Complacency 26

16. Confession 27

17. Critics 30

18. The Declaration 31

19. The Defining Factor of Your Life 32

20. The Definition of Who You Are 33

21. Dignity and How to Get It 34

22. What to Do When You Feel Like Dirt 36

23. The Embarrassment of Being a Christian . . . 37

24. Evil 38

25. Fame 39

26. A Flight Attendant's Prayer 40

27. How to Have Friends 43

28. A Friend of Sinners 44

29. A Gentle Answer 45

30. God Is 46

31. Grace in the Growth 47

32. Gratitude 49

33. Great Gain 50

34. The Hematoma 52

35. Honor 55

36. How to Be Humble 57

37. How to Get What You Want 58

38. How Long It Takes to Write a Book 60

39. How to Tell a Wise Man from a Fool
    in Two Easy Lessons 62

40. Humility Comes Before Honor 65

41. Ten Things to Look for in a Husband 66

42. Inside Image 69

43. Intuition 70

44. Jesus as a Swearword 71

45. A Container for Joy 72

46. The Joyful Fanatic 73

47. Just As I Am 74

48. Journaling 75

49. Judging Others 76

50. Acting Justly Is a Scary Thing 77

51. Knowing God 79

52. The Last Week Is the Hardest 81

53. Laughing at Yourself 82

54. Learning 84

55. The Lesson of the Fussy Housekeeper

(from the Story of Mary and Martha) 85

56. It's Better to Be Lonely Single

Than Lonely Married 87

57. The Lost Child 89

58. Lust 92

59. The Marriage Bed 94

60. The Most Important Thing to Look

for in a Marriage Partner 95

61. How to Grow a Miracle 97

62. The Most Common Mistake 98

63. Mourning What Is Lost 99

64. When No Is an Answer 100

65. Old Furniture 101

66. A Parent's Love 102

67. Perspective 104

68. Pinching People to Jesus 105

69. Pleasing God 108

70. Pleasure 109

71. Possessions 110

72. You Can Pray About Anything 111

73. A Twelve-Word Prayer 113

74. Prayer Is Stronger than Magic 114

75. Pride 116

76. In Prison with Grandma 117

77. The Benefit of Keeping Quiet 120

78. It's Not Rejection; It's Redirection 121

79. What to Do When You Murder

    Your Reputation 122

80. How to Be a Saint 125

81. Seeking 126

82. The Self-Made Man 127

83. Sex and Your Soul 128

84. Why We Sing 130

85. The Small Business of Marriage 131

86. Solar Power 133

87. Time 134

88. Your Tragedy Is Not Your Identity 136

89. How to Be Unique 138

90. There Will Always Be Things
    We Don't Understand 139

91. The Valentine's Day Glow 140

92. Victory 143

93. Vision 144

94. Waiting: The Story of My Life 145

95. What God Chooses 148

96. What You Don't Know Can Hurt You ... 149

97. Why Things Always Go Wrong 152

98. Wisdom 155

99. Words That Will Change Your Life 156

100. Worry 157

101. You Will Always Be Ridiculed
     by Someone 159

Acknowledgments 160

INTRODUCTION

Being a part-time hypochondriac, I often grieve my imminent death. One day, while mourning my life cut short by the impact of my disease du jour, I decided to write something to leave as a legacy to my survivors.

I wrote what I'm most familiar with: simple lessons gleaned from a lifetime of reading the best-selling book of all time, the Bible. I illustrated the lessons the only way I know how—with true stories from my life. Yes, the stories are all true, but they didn't all happen back to back, as you are reading them here; they happened over the course of years.

I'm praying for each reader of this book. This is my prayer: *Lord, let them be encouraged and inspired, and if neither of those, may they just have a good laugh, which is also therapeutic.*

ACTIONS AND
WHAT FOLLOW THEM

Feelings follow actions. You go out for a run, you feel good. You hurt someone, you feel bad. This was brought home to me in a personal way when I asked my husband once why he regularly told me he loved me.

"Feelings follow actions," he said. "I tell you I love you, and it reminds me that's what I am called to do: love you. It brings into focus my actions and promotes that feeling in me again." (Now if that isn't the explanation of an aerospace engineer, I don't know what is.)

My husband is right. Feelings follow actions. Determine this day how you want to feel and direct your actions to that effect.

ADORATION

I t takes the heart of a child to adore. That is, to recognize something totally outside yourself while
holding that thing close to your heart. *O come, let us
adore him...*

THE AVAILABILITY
OF GOD

God is at once available and mysterious. We may find him, but we never find him out.

This is one reason heaven will be wonderful. The facets of goodness are never-ending. There is always more to discover.

BEING BORN AGAIN

I t was in the spring of my forty-ninth year that I was born again geographically. That is to say, we moved from Seattle to Savannah.

Before that—having lived twenty-two years of my life in and around Seattle—I would have told you with the confidence of a vision-impaired fool that there was no better place to live.

I would have pointed out our mountain ranges, our evergreens, and our coffee. I would have mentioned the national pastime in Seattle, which is walking in the rain. And I would have told you how all my colleagues agree with me. We were confident in our geographic superiority. The Midwest was a place to leave, the East was a place to visit, and the South, well, the South was to be avoided at all costs.

It isn't that we just disliked the South. We hated the South as only someone who has never experienced something but has been prejudiced against it can hate. We had read books, we had listened to our parents, and we had watched television. One thing we knew for a fact: It was hot and humid in the South. It was almost never hot in Seattle. (And we didn't consider the constant mist from gloomy skies to be humidity.)

Then came the fateful day. My husband—the major breadwinner in our home—quit the Seattle job he'd had for ten years and accepted the job of his dreams in Savannah, Georgia. I wanted to protest, but the look in my husband's eyes when he came out of the interviews was too much like that of a little boy who'd been offered a new race car.

I set out to move to a place I knew would be similar to purgatory.

We landed at the Savannah airport, and I fell in love with the airport. I loved how small it was and how it also served Hilton Head, South Carolina. I loved how it rented golf clubs as well as cars because this place is Golf Heaven. Then we drove to downtown Savannah and I was stunned.

It was the prettiest city I'd ever seen, and I've been around the world—Rome, Paris, Madrid, London, Zurich (all the while carefully avoiding the South).

The weather was perfect. The month was March. It was seventy-five degrees with a slight breeze off the ocean. The city was laid out around shaded parks and buildings that were some of the oldest in the United States. Giant two-hundred-year-old oak trees stretched out branches that formed canopies down wide walkways. The Spanish moss swaying from branches was so picturesque it appeared to have been placed by a set designer. I stood for a minute taking it all in and began humming the tune to "Georgia on My Mind." (The whole time I lived in Washington State, I don't ever remember singing its state song.)

We have now lived just outside Savannah for more than one year, and I never want to leave. I love this place. I love the two months of cold, the two months of hot, and mostly I love the eight months of perfect. I love the beach—minutes from our home with the white sand and the eighty-degree water. I love the no traffic and the green trees lining every major road from here to Hilton Head. I love the forests and how easy it is to drive anywhere you want. Did I mention I love the no traffic?

The way I approached moving to Savannah is the way some people approach the idea of Christianity. They have read about it and think they know what it is like. They say there is no way they are going to be born again spiritually.

I understand that thinking. I was just as adamant about something I was sure wasn't for me.

BELIEF

My favorite eight-word prayer is "Lord, I believe; help me with my unbelief."

BEST FRIENDS

Some friends are just friends because it's best. That's why they are called best friends. I would say one of the chief things I look for in a best friend is independence. Just as the best marriages are made when two people who have existed apart from each other find that when they come together they each bring something so wonderful that the whole is greater than the parts—so it is with a friendship. Nothing kills a friendship quicker than a clinger or a needy leech. Of course, in my past, I've been both of those things to other people. I suppose that's why I like the movie *What About Bob?* so much. It describes what happens when a needy leech wants to be a friend, and what happens when one tries to be gentle with such a person. I can relate to both characters.

My husband, who is more stable than I am and has never been associated with anyone like Bob, nor has he ever been a "Bob" himself, doesn't find that movie humorous at all.

BITTER INTO SWEET

I suspect the large chain bookstore scheduled my very first book-signing ever because I promised them I could sell four hundred copies in one day. I had no clue that was a high number. I thought it sounded good.

"Wow," said the manager. "That's a lot for a first-time author, at least at this store. Our average author sells ten to twelve copies at a signing—unless you're a movie star or world famous."

"Well…" I said, musing on the fact that only about two people in the entire universe knew me as an author. "Let's change it to one hundred copies." Then I said, "You order one hundred. And what doesn't sell, I'll buy."

I didn't tell my husband I'd bet our house payment against sales of my book. The signing was booked for September 29, 2001. This was mid-August 2001. I had six weeks to prepare for it. What could go wrong?

Everything, it seems. Here are the first five things:

1. In July, I bought an ad in a media publication, describing myself as a fun guest. The ad

was to get to all the local radio stations mid-morning of September 11, 2001.

2. In early September, my publisher informed me that my books had been confiscated by the printer.

3. Then, of course, September 11 hit and life as we know it stopped. My signing had been scheduled for September 29. I didn't cancel it. September 15, I heard that the new printer had smeared the first print-run.

4. Forty-eight hours before my signing, we heard one hundred books were being shipped directly to the store. Twenty-four hours before the signing, we had books but no buyers because…

5. After we heard we might not have books, *nobody* wanted to advertise what might not happen.

The only person I told about the signing-that-was-going-bad was a neighbor of mine, someone who didn't go to church and told me she wasn't a believer in God. She listened to everything that had gone wrong and laughed at all the right places.

Then the day of the signing came, and I don't know how, but we sold out—108 books in three hours. We sold to people I'd never seen or met. Some of them came in clutching an article from the paper that was almost a month old. Some of them saw me in the mall fifteen minutes before the signing when I was begging people to come into the bookstore. Some of them had secretly listened as I did my reading before the signing for an audience of two.

There was one person I recognized in the audience. It was my neighbor. The one who told me she didn't believe in God. She said she came because there was no advance publicity and she was concerned no one would come. She bought seven copies of my book. "Christmas gifts," she said.

When I visited her later, she told me she had stayed up till 11 P.M. that night reading my book. She looked at me and asked, "What kind of Christian are you?"

"I'm the basic kind," I said. "I simply believe Jesus is who he said he was!" I shared with her a few of the outlandish claims of Christ. And I told her I believed them all.

She asked me to explain about why Christ had to die. I did, and I asked her if she'd like to pray with me. She did.

And that is how God used the whole five things that went wrong for his good. If everything had gone right from the beginning, I might never have talked to my neighbor about the bitter bother. And she might never have seen God. The God who takes what is bitter and turns it into something sweet.

BLESSING US

Sometimes God blesses us by making us uncomfortable. He'll allow trouble to enter our sanctuary—the place that used to be perfect for us and in which we would like to stay hunkered down against anything that's scary. He'll allow so much trouble that one day we can't stand it anymore and we leave what is familiar and move into a place we would never have visited if we had remained trouble-free. In this way, God blesses us with trouble, stirring up our nests as an eagle stirs up her nest.

When an eagle builds her nest, she hunts for soft pieces of cloth and feathers to lay a place for her babies to be born. But under the soft layer, she will first put down what you would never suspect from a loving parent. She buries a layer of sharp, painful, cutting objects. Things like broken glass, twigs, thorns, all manner of hurtful items. Then over those items, she puts the soft part.

The babies' first experience is soft, and they are comforted and nourished. Then when the eagle decides the time is right, she stirs up the nest. She digs her talons deep under all the soft and stirs up the awful, sharp pieces. She allows her babies to hop around in pain until finally those babies are so troubled they can't take it anymore and they leave the nest by hopping right to the very edge.

Then they are where the eagle wants them. She gives them a push, and they fall into the place they would never have gone on their own. Before they fall too far, the eagle swoops down and catches them on her wings and carries them back up to where they are safe. And then she drops them again, until they learn to fly. Learning to fly would be out of the question if the eagle left the decision to the babies. They would never choose discomfort.

Is God stirring up your nest today? Are you uncomfortable and getting jabbed while staying in a place that used to be perfect for you? Perhaps it is God's way of getting you ready for a place that is better than you could imagine.

BOLDNESS

Have you ever seen a young child who knows her mother loves her go to talk with her mother in a frank manner? This is how God wants us to approach him. Bold and humble at the same time. Boldness is not the opposite of humility; it can, in fact, be a sign of it.

So, let us approach the throne with boldness.

BRAGGING

Proverbs 27:2 says, "Don't praise yourself; let others do it!" (NLT). There is something very practical about that verse. When we hear someone brag on themselves, we don't count their words credible. But when someone else praises them, we listen.

THE CHILD WHO HAD NO MANNERS (AND SHE WAS DIRTY, TOO)

What if a child came to your church and you knew the child's mother was a single woman who worked in a bar? What if you knew that mother had been married several times and had not used good judgment on any of the marriages? What if the child was not well-dressed or very clean, had no manners, and was loud and disruptive? What if you knew the mother took the child to church only so she could have some time off, and the child seemed to want to cause trouble just to get attention?

How would you act toward that child? Would you be kind? Would you treat that child so special she'd beg to be able to come back? Would you make that child feel as important as another kid with nice clothes from a solid home, who was clean and used manners and smelled wonderful? Would you use the extra patience it would take to get to the heart of the problem with that child? Would you love her so she could understand what the Bible means by "he quiets us with his love"?

I'm asking that because, years ago, I was that dirty child from the broken home. I was the child that caused everyone to shake their heads when my mom dropped me off at the local church on Sundays and Wednesdays. I was the child with no manners. I was the child you would have voted most likely to fail.

But in the church where my mom dropped me off, I discovered a nurturing group of people who seemed to think I was worth something. Sunday school teachers who went the second mile for me when I had no way of paying them for the first. And church people who told me stories about characters in the Bible who seemed to have it worse than I did.

First, there was this guy, Joseph, who was dropped in a well by his brothers. This other guy, David, was hiding from a crazy king who wanted to kill him. And there was this girl, Rahab, who had been known to work in a job that wasn't respected, yet who ended up being mentioned as one of the most faithful people in the Bible. Another girl, Esther, whose parents were nowhere around, was selected to accomplish a mission that saved the lives of all God's people.

In Sunday school lessons, I learned of a God who could use anybody or anything committed to him. A God who could take something awful and completely change it so you'd never recognize what it used to be.

And I learned from the way my teachers treated me that God's view of things was different from the world's. That God saw everyone as having been at one time on the "wrong side of the tracks," and what was important was not where we'd been but where we were headed.

The little church I went to as a child had people in it who seemed to feel that if they acted out God's love toward a small, dirty child from a broken home, it could make a difference.

And it has.

Love one another. As I have loved you.
—JOHN 13:34

CHOICES

I wish that when I was small someone had impressed upon me the importance of choices. Each choice we make is like a play in a giant Scrabble game. Each choice influences all other choices.

In case you were wondering, there are no small choices. They are all huge. So what we need here is a great director. Some great director of life, a counselor to advise us on the choices that will be best for us.

God provides that. He has left us a counselor, the Spirit of truth. But we must *choose* to follow the prompting of that Spirit.

THE VIEW OF THE COMMON MAN

I am a common flight attendant, and that's how I wanted to write this book, from the view of a common worker. But I am not just a common worker—I am someone who has been in the presence of the King.

That is the most amazing thing about Christianity. It invites us common folk—flight attendants, factory workers, teachers, garbage collectors—to enter by faith the room of heaven.

A room that is *holy*, where God himself dwells and waits patiently for visits from his children.

The knowledge of the secrets of the kingdom of God has been given to you.
—LUKE 8:10

COMMUNICATION

L et your 'Yes' be yes, and your 'No,' no" (James 5:12).
I never paid much attention to this verse until a few months after my first book came out. It was ten weeks before Memorial Day when I received an e-mail request to speak at a church that is about two hours from my home. They wanted me to speak on a Saturday night in April to a dinner of about forty women.

I didn't really want to do it. It takes me a full day to prepare one talk. And this would also involve several hours' packing and travel, just to speak to a small group of people.

But I didn't have the courage to say no, so I wrote back and said I'd love to come—and hoped they'd lose the e-mail. I said yes when I meant no.

Then, weeks later, another e-mail arrived from them, mentioning that they expected me to stay over and be the speaker at the Sunday morning service as well.

They had to be kidding! I was busy at the time I received the invitation and didn't have time to properly respond and say, "Are you nuts? No!" So I said nothing. Didn't even answer the e-mail, hoping my silence would speak my no.

Well, they took my silence for a yes.

And then they changed the date from April to the end of May. Memorial Day weekend.

They sent me an e-mail in April informing me of the date change. And they wanted to know, would I still be interested? No! I was not interested. It was *Memorial Day.* My husband gets a rare weekend off. I wanted to be with him. But, again, do you think I said no?

No! *Wimping out* is what I did! I didn't want to hurt their feelings. So, instead of saying either yes or no, I *again* ignored the e-mail, hoping that if I didn't respond, they would think, *Well, she must mean no.*

Three days before Memorial Day, an e-mail arrived in which they told me how excited they were that I was going to be the speaker at their church for Memorial Day weekend. Both Saturday night and Sunday morning, and would I be available for lunch Sunday afternoon?

I wanted to say, "No. I don't want to spend my whole Memorial Day weekend, which could be a mini-vacation with my family, with people I don't know." But, instead, I didn't say anything. Which they took as a yes.

So, I did what I had to do; I showed up and spoke the Saturday night before Memorial Day and the Sunday morning as well, and I stayed for lunch. And you know what? I got blessed. And even my husband and daughter, who came with me, enjoyed themselves.

I also got blessed in a way I didn't expect. I learned from this experience that it's not kind to others not to be honest in your speech. Although it all worked out well, I should have told these people the truth from the beginning.

And believe me, I have learned my lesson. If I don't feel the engagement is good for me, or a good time for me to be away from my family, I'm going to say no. From this day forward, my yes will be yes and my no will be no.

Let your yes be yes and your no be no. It will end up making you happier in the long run, and it's more honoring to those who want the truth from you.

COMPLACENCY

Familiarity doesn't breed contempt as much as it breeds complacency, and complacency is sometimes more cruel than contempt.

CONFESSION

Someone once said that confession is good for the soul. I can tell you it's good for my soul to hear others confess that they struggle with the same things I do. And it's good for my soul to tell you some of the things I struggle with.

What do I struggle with? Well, here's one thing: I struggle with trying to keep our house in a state in which my husband can at least walk through it.

Today, for example, my husband asked if I wouldn't mind just clearing a path to the bed. I said, "Why don't you stand at the door and jump in, like I do?" He said, "I've done that for years. Tonight, I want to walk."

So, honoring him, I went into our room where the piles of clothes looked as if they had erupted from Mount Dresser, and I began to hang things up. After hanging up one item, I realized this could take forever, and my husband needed to go to sleep soon. So, I kicked clothes, magazines, and old candy wrappers aside to clear a two-foot-wide walkway from the door to our bed. And then, going the extra mile, I cleared another path from the bed to the bathroom.

It looked like the Red Sea had parted. Except instead of walls of water, there were walls of clothes on either side of the cleared part.

Now, you would think this effort on my part would have resulted in praise and adoration from my husband, but as soon as he got into the bed, he jumped back out, holding what looked like a crumpled bag of microwave popcorn.

Apparently, I'd had a little snack in bed and had forgotten to clean up the remains. He ripped the blankets off the bed and started sweeping the sheet with his arms as if he was looking for land mines. He started mumbling about kernels and salt. It was then that I remembered that the bag had spilled and I hadn't had time to clean it up. Tom said he thought he had noticed the same salty feeling in bed the night before. (Okay, so I'm not perfect.)

Maybe you have a fussy husband like I do. Or maybe you're like me, and you fail to see what the big deal is. I like to think of my messy house as a sign of my genius. I'm sure as you're reading this you are thinking, *No honey, it's a sign you're a slob.* But think about it: Einstein didn't ever see anything but what he was working on or thinking about. He didn't even dress decently. That's how I am. I am a writer. I am continually thinking about a piece of writing that I am developing or want to develop. Not about trivial things, like did I get the lid back on the mustard or what happens when you leave a spilled bag of potato chips on the living room floor for a month? (No, we do not have bugs. We have our house sprayed. Thank God.)

Anyway, my husband said he couldn't stand it anymore. I had just sent off my second book to the publisher. My husband said that before I start another book, he wants to be able to move freely through our home without fear of falling debris or falling over debris. So, I promised him I'd clean it.

Now, I'm not detail-oriented with cleaning-type things. This could take a week or a year or something. That's why I'm confessing this to you. The Bible says to confess our shortcomings and pray for each other. Perhaps you'll pray for me.

And don't tell me to hire a cleaning lady. I've already been turned down by two. They said, "Honey, we don't clean houses this messy."

CRITICS

C ritics can be fools, even when they have been ele-
vated to their position by some impressive officers.

THE DECLARATION

The heavens declare the glory of God;
>   the skies proclaim the work of his hands.
Day after day they pour forth speech;
>   night after night they display knowledge.
There is no speech or language
>   where their voice is not heard.
Their voice goes out into all the earth,
>   their words to the ends of the world.
>   (Psalm 19:1-4)

To declare something means "to reveal or make manifest, or show." I find it interesting that the heavens *declare*, they *shout*, the Glory of God, and the whole firmament shows his handiwork. I like the idea that each day and night speak of the glory of God and that speech goes on 24/7. In every language, every tribe, every nation.

THE DEFINING FACTOR
OF YOUR LIFE

Discerning truth from falsehood will be the defining factor of your life. That's why Proverbs is such an important book; it tells you how to become a discerning person.

THE DEFINITION
OF WHO YOU ARE

In Mark 3:21, it says that Jesus' family thought he was nuts. Or actually, "out of his mind." That is a comfort to me. Sometimes families are wrong.

DIGNITY AND
HOW TO GET IT

Dignity is not for sale anywhere, yet everyone wants to have it. The dictionary defines it as the state of being worthy of respect or esteem. Babies are born with it. All babies are born with so much dignity, in fact, that complete strangers express awe when a baby comes into view. And what's interesting about babies having dignity is that they can't even control their own bodily functions or clean up after themselves. So we learn from them that dignity has nothing to do with how able-bodied we are.

If babies everywhere are born with dignity and adults everywhere want to be known for having dignity, what happens between our babyhood and our adulthood that results in a loss of dignity? Well, first I'll tell you what doesn't happen. What doesn't happen is nobody takes it from us. It's impossible to steal anyone's dignity.

No, what happens is we lose it by making choices we know are wrong. Bad choices. Choices we know go against God's law that is written on our hearts and conscience. That law that tells us, "Don't do it." We ignore that law and think there will be no consequences, but there *are* consequences. Each time we do something we know is wrong, we lose a bit more dignity, until one day some of us wake up barren, with no self-respect left, no sense of worth or self-esteem. Our souls (the soul is the container for dignity) are in need of restoration. (This is one reason the line in Psalm 23 is quoted so often: "He restores my soul.")

Is it possible to get dignity back after you've lost it? Yes. How? By beginning to make choices for good over evil. It's never too late to begin to choose right over wrong.

There was a man who waited until the last minute of his life to do something right. He was one of the men being crucified next to Christ. At the last minute, he stood up for Jesus and told the other tormentor to bug off. That one simple act brought dignity to the dying criminal. And as he drew his last breath, he did it with dignity.

If you make a choice for dignity before your last breath, you will have a chance to rebuild what you lost earlier. And dignity restored is a beautiful thing. Have you ever seen someone who turned their life around? Who went through a program or treatment and stopped making decisions they knew were wrong? Those people get their dignity back, and it's almost as if they are new babies—born again.

So the choice for dignity is ours—and a big choice it is too.

WHAT TO DO WHEN
YOU FEEL LIKE DIRT

When you feel like dirt, there is only one thing to do. Don't just lie there wallowing. Raise your arms to the One who will pick you up and make something with what you give him. Give yourself to the One who once used a little dust to make something so valuable he sent his Son to redeem it.

The LORD God formed the man
from the dust of the ground.
—GENESIS 2:7

THE EMBARRASSMENT
OF BEING A CHRISTIAN

I am not ashamed of the gospel" (Romans 1:16).
I used to read that verse and think, *I am. I am
ashamed*. But it's more like being embarrassed by it. It's
like being in love. If you've ever been in love, you know
it can be incredibly embarrassing. When you are first in
love, all you talk about is the attributes of the one who
has captivated you. And when you are in love, you see
everything in light of your new love.

The difference is that being in love on earth isn't
always a lasting thing, but being in love with Jesus *is* a
lasting thing. The joy from this love relationship is so
much deeper than anything on earth, it makes for much
more embarrassing behavior. I suppose the only answer
is to be so in love that you don't look back, so glowing
from being in the presence of Jesus, your lover, that you
don't even care what the world thinks. That's the only
answer I know.

EVIL

S ome people think they can leave the side of good and go hang out on the side of evil for a while, and then come back to good. The danger is this: The further we go down one path, the easier it becomes to run to the end.

FAME

When my daughter was almost five, she came up to me and asked me why my picture was in the paper. I told her it was because I was famous that day. She paused for a minute and then told me she wanted her picture in the paper as well. I asked her why, and she said, "I just think it would be nice."

I'm wondering if she thought as I once did, that fame would make her feel more loved. It doesn't work that way. The love of family makes us feel loved. The love of fans isn't the same because we know those people don't really know us. It's the love of those who know us that means the most.

A Flight
Attendant's Prayer

D o not worry" (Matthew 6:25, 6:31, and 6:34; Mark 13:11; Luke 12:22 and 12:29). Ten days after September 11, 2001, I was reading this command (it appears all through the Bible) and I realized that I'd been ignoring it. Okay, flat out disobeying it. Do not worry. It is repeated in more ways and in more places than I've listed above. "For I am the LORD, your God, who takes hold of your right hand and says to you, 'Do not fear; I will help you'" (Isaiah 41:13).

Now, the logical left side of my brain knows that God holds my hand and will help me. But the week of September 11, I went into right-brain mode, which doesn't care a whit about what logic says. Right brain said: *Freak out.*

By the end of the week of September 11, I was depressed and fearful and lashing out at anyone who wasn't as worried as I was. My husband—the recipient of some of my rudeness—pointed out this was not effective communication and had to stop. So, I went to the God who allows us to bring all our sins to him ("'Come now and let us reason together,' says the Lord"), and I spent some time reasoning the effects of worry.

I came away with an insight into why worry isn't a good thing but concern is okay. *Concern* is positive, leading to action born out of wise counsel. Worry, on the other hand, is negative and leads to depression, which is debilitating, or to rash behavior born out of irrational fear.

So, I got that whole worry thing taken care of... until my job called and said I needed to report to work. Now, most writers have other jobs. My job is the greatest of jobs for a writer who likes time off and international travel. And normally it's a safe job. I'm a flight attendant.

Do not worry. *Excuse me, Lord, do you realize what I do for a living?* Do not worry. *Excuse me, Lord, they took over four airplanes.* Do not worry. *I'm sorry, Lord, my job wants me to fly twelve flights in three days and I think...I don't think, I know, that I'm freaking out here. I'm so nervous, I could vomit on a passenger.* Do not fear.

There is a prayer in the Bible called the Lord's Prayer. For those of us who don't like to get creative in our prayers, it was offered as a model. There is one line in it that got me through my first days back at work as a flight attendant after September 11. The line is found in Matthew 6:13 (KJV), and it says, "Deliver us from evil." I prayed those four words over and over as I boarded passengers, served them a smile and a beverage, watched them deplane and board yet another plane. Deliver us from evil. *Yes, Lord, even the evil of worry and fear.*

Perhaps you have a problem with worry as well. Or fear. Perhaps you'll join me this week in praying these four words: Deliver us from evil.

HOW TO HAVE FRIENDS

He who has friends must show himself friendly." I used to study popular people and wonder how they got that way. This saying explains it. If you are friendly to others, you will have friends. It's simple but effective.

A FRIEND OF SINNERS

Some friendships are heavy in depth and light in length.

Some seem to go on forever in the space of a moment.

"I have called you friends," Jesus said, and we are honored because a family is something you are born into, but a friend is something you choose.

A GENTLE ANSWER

A gentle answer turns away wrath, but a harsh word stirs up anger" (Proverbs 15:1). My husband, Tom, is the master of the gentle answer. Once when I was in a rage at him and I was out of town, I sent him an e-mail telling him that he was treating me like an idiot and I was furious about it. "I am not an idiot," I said, "and I won't be treated like one."

Within minutes of sending the e-mail, I called Tom on the phone and said, "Did you get my e-mail?"

He answered very gently, "Yes, but I have one question. What's an *eye-dot?*"

Apparently, I, who can't spell under the best of circumstances and really can't spell when I am angry, had spelled *idiot, idot.* Repeatedly throughout the e-mail, I had written, "I am not an *idot* and I won't be treated like an *idot* and you are treating me like an *idot* and I won't stand for it." I was laughing so hard at the end of Tom's reading back my e-mail to me that my anger was turned away. A gentle answer turns away wrath.

GOD IS

Yes, God is good and loving and just and kind and awesome and a very present help in times of trouble. But before he is any of those things, he simply *is*.

Your whole life will be lived on one side of this truth or the other. Either you will live as if he is or as if he isn't. Some days will contain actions that seem to be born of both beliefs.

GRACE IN THE GROWTH

Our friend Jack used to say to his three-year-old daughter when she spilled her milk, "You are acting just like a three-year-old." And when the child was five and did something exasperating, Jack would say, "You are acting just like a five-year-old." By saying this, Jack was reminding himself that children will act their age. When Jack was young, parents everywhere used to scold their children for not acting their age. What they meant was that children should act older than their age, use a maturity beyond their age.

Expect your child—or any child—to act his or her age. Yes, the goal is to grow in maturity. But a three-year-old who explores and touches and spills things isn't being a bad child; he is acting his age. He can't be expected to use the judgment of someone ten times his age, or even someone twice his age.

I was reminded of this last night when our neighbors were over with their four-year-old rambunctious little boy. He threw sand. He left the back door open.

On one of his trips through our house to the bathroom, he climbed up on the leather couch and got sand everywhere. Then as he left our home and walked down our front driveway, he reached out to grab a handful of blooms off a flowering bush and knelt down to pound the top of a solar light that lines the driveway. It was a cheap light and he broke the top off. He wasn't being a bad kid; he was just being four. I wanted to yell and tell him to get away from our things. But then I remembered that people are more important than things. He was just acting his age.

And I should expect that. It's part of grace. A grace extended to us by God as well. God expects us to mature, but along the growth process he remembers what we are and how old we are, and he extends the grace of growth.

GRATITUDE

Gratitude changes an attitude faster than anything I've seen. That's why God tells us to give thanks—often.

GREAT GAIN

My husband's favorite verse is 1 Timothy 6:6: "Godliness with contentment is great gain." It doesn't just say godliness is great gain, or contentment is great gain, but godliness with contentment is great gain.

Godliness comes to those who live in right relationship to God. And great gain is what makes you succeed. So, it's a good thing to want both of these.

We recently watched the movie *A Beautiful Mind,* and one line in the movie struck me. The main character, John Nash, was answering a question about how he dealt with harmful images that would sometimes come to his mind. He said, "It's like a diet of the mind." He had to resolve in his heart, mind, and soul to put himself on a mental diet. To cut out things that would not allow him to move forward in the direction of health.

I would say if we want godliness with contentment, which is great gain, we need to heed that advice. For example, in the most practical sense, if I want to assist my mind in staying content, I have to stay out of shopping malls. It's like a diet of the senses. Shopping malls exist to breed discontentment. They will tell you they are there to make you content, but actually they are there to show you what you don't have and make you think you need it. If you stay in them long enough—for me it's about five minutes—you will begin to feel inadequate with how you look and wonder, as I do, if that new hat would be the thing to bring contentment.

Write this verse down and carry it with you the next time you have to go shopping: "Godliness with contentment is great gain."

THE HEMATOMA

A lot of people say that perception is reality, but I know that sometimes perception has nothing at all to do with reality.

For example, I like to read medical books, and sometimes when I'm reading those books, I begin to imagine I have the disease I'm reading about. I'll read about a disease with symptoms of a tingling big toe, and suddenly my big toe is tingling. It doesn't take much to make the leap from a symptom of the disease to planning my funeral. All based on a false perception.

However, there was one day when the reading of my medical books paid off. On that day I made the alarming discovery of a hematoma on my baby's leg. Mandy was five months old at the time. I'd laid her down for the evening, and when she woke up the next morning there it was: the ugliest hematoma ever. So dark purple and clotted with blood you could hardly see the skin. It was a quarter-inch in diameter and sticking up like a wart. A hematoma is defined in the medical dictionary as "a localized collection of blood, usually clotted in an organ, space, or tissue due to a break in the wall of a blood vessel." I had never seen one this thick with blood and this firm. I bathed Mandy with a sponge, carefully avoiding the hematoma. I was afraid to touch it. When I called the pediatrician's office and told them what was happening, they were sufficiently alarmed to get me in right away.

The expert doctor examined the hematoma from all angles. He swabbed it a few times and studied it some more. Then, to my horror, he began discussing his career and the importance of documenting such an unusual hematoma for the medical records. He spoke of doing a paper on this and getting published and recognized.

I felt I was in some kind of a nightmare in which the mother of the child only wants to know how we are going to prevent future breaks in her daughter's blood vessels and the doctor wants to get famous from the event.

But I was too stunned to protest; when the doctor went to get his camera, I went mute. He came back in and positioned my daughter's leg under the bright lights of the camera. Then he swabbed the hematoma one more time. And it came off. That's when I realized it was a gummy bear. A grape gummy bear. Actually half of a grape gummy bear. I'd been eating them over my daughter's crib and apparently I had bit one in half and the other half had gone into the folds of her blanket and adhered to her leg where it had sealed itself by the warmth of her body and hardened as it was exposed to air.

The doctor's warm lights had shown on the leg so long they had softened the hardened candy and revealed it for what it was.

I yelled, "Oh, it's a gummy bear! A grape gummy bear!" The doctor lowered his camera.

I've never seen red blush of embarrassment rise on a man's face as I saw it rise on the face of this pediatrician who was going to be famous one minute for a medical discovery and who now realized he'd be immortalized as a fool. At least he put his camera away when it was made obvious that what we had perceived wasn't reality.

I figure there are a whole lot of people in the world building a case against faith on the basis of half a grape gummy bear stuck to the leg. They think their case will advance them in good repute when, in fact, one day they will be exposed as fools.

Perception is not always reality, no matter how educated your perception is. Sometimes things just aren't what they seem.

HONOR

My picture had been on the front page of our local paper for several weeks in a row. It was advertising my weekly column, and then inside the paper, where my column was posted, there was a larger picture of me. If you have your picture in the paper long enough and often enough, people begin to recognize you. Plus I did some local book-signings and speaking, so I was getting famous—in the small county where I live.

On Monday my daughter and I were getting ready to leave the local McDonald's. As we left, I put my drink on top of my car, unlocked the door, and put my daughter in. Then as I got into the car, an older customer came running out of the restaurant to tell me not to drive away because the drink was still on top of my car.

I thanked him and then he just stood there, getting that look in his eye that people get when they recognize me from my picture. "I know who you are," he said, "but you don't remember me." Then we chatted a bit more and I got into the car where Mandy was waiting.

As I pulled away, I was sort of basking in the glow of fame—in the fact that it had happened, after thirty years of effort! I finally had a book out, was a newspaper columnist, and was getting recognized for what I love to do. I decided to share all this with my preschool daughter.

"Mandy," I said, "that man recognized me because I'm famous! Mommy's a famous author!"

Mandy pulled her thumb out of her mouth and gave me a "don't be ridiculous" stare.

"Mom," she said, "he recognized you from McDonald's. He's seen you in there before." She put her thumb back in her mouth. Case closed.

An author is not without honor, except in her own family and her own car.

HOW TO BE HUMBLE

How does one get humble? By casting all one's care on God. This means admitting that we can't handle life as God can. You wouldn't believe how hard it is for some people to admit they need help from someone they aren't sure exists.

How does humility happen? It happens when we humble ourselves. The Bible says humble yourselves under the mighty hand of God.

Why does God want us to humble ourselves? So he can exalt us. *What? He wants us to humble ourselves so he can exalt us?* Yes, that's the kind of God he is, one who exalts the humble.

Can we ask God to help us humble ourselves? Of course. The Bible says pray about everything, and you can pray about anything. In fact, asking God for help is the first step on the road to humility.

HOW TO GET
WHAT YOU WANT

In John 16:24 Jesus said, "Ask and you will receive." I love this verse because it tells us how to get what we want. I hate this verse for the same reason. I don't like to be blamed for my own lack of things.

But enough about who is to blame. Here's the answer to getting what we want: Ask. It's so simple. My daughter taught me this anew one day when she was four years old. Somehow she had figured out that she didn't have to have just what was my idea for a meal. She could suggest her ideas. And I would listen to her. She told me one morning that she wanted toast with syrup. I asked her again, "Toast, in the toaster, on a plate, with syrup?"

"Yes!" she said and went over each detail of how to make it.

So, I did make it—figuring that she must have seen something on television and this was her version of the French toast I grew up with. An easier version to make, I might add.

After she'd requested that meal for three mornings in a row, I thought of something. She got the meal she wanted because she asked for it, and she asked specifically. She didn't demand it, she didn't whine about it, she knew that I love her so much I want to give her the desires of her heart.

HOW LONG IT TAKES
TO WRITE A BOOK

People often ask me how long it took to write my first book. I mean it's a simple book, fewer than two hundred pages, with some pages only containing a paragraph or sentence of original text. Well, the answer is forty-nine years and eighteen weeks. The eighteen weeks is approximately how many hours I spent composing the text that represented the first forty-nine years of life and study.

If the key to great writing is to discover your passion and get to know your passion, I'd have to say the getting-to-know-your-passion is the part that takes the longest. I knew my passion was to share my faith in a way that didn't sound boring. But after discovering my passion, it took time to *know* it, to really understand it. I had to study the Bible for years and meditate on it for hours a day, many days of the month. Months turned into years—of going to church, learning from Bible teachers, going to Bible school, and teaching Sunday school. In order to purée the spiritual principles, I had to first know them.

Sometimes, there is no substitute for time. I hate that, but it's true. Most authors weren't always that way. It takes time to be an author, usually more than a day.

HOW TO TELL A WISE
MAN FROM A FOOL IN
TWO EASY LESSONS

Proverbs 29:11 says, "A fool gives full vent to his
anger, but a wise man keeps himself under control."
I am not the most self-controlled person in the world.
When I'm under stress, as I was last night, acting like a
fool comes, well, naturally.

Tom, Mandy, and I were returning from a whirl-
wind weekend visiting Tom's parents in Lincoln,
Nebraska. We had boarded an already delayed flight in
Omaha and then sat on the tarmac at our connection in
Atlanta. Consequently we had only minutes to make our
connecting flight to Savannah. That flight, the last one
of the day, wouldn't get us home until close to midnight,
but if we didn't catch it, we'd be sleeping in the airport.

The flight attendant hadn't allowed passengers to
get up and use the bathroom while we sat on an active

runway in Atlanta, and Mandy was letting us know she needed a bathroom. *Now.*

As soon as the attendants opened the airplane doors, we were off that plane in Atlanta, and Tom raced on ahead with Mandy to get her to the restroom.

I was left carrying the luggage, and being tired and cranky, I semiyelled for Tom to wait a minute. He shook his head no. I lost it. Then the thought (which seemed like a good idea at the time) came to me that I should give full vent to my anger and screech at the top of my lungs for Tom to stop.

The airport was crowded. I have a loud voice. The fool in me was urging me on. This would teach Tom a lesson. Oh yeah. I was on the edge of "going for the full vent" when I remembered—I worked for the airline. Officials of my airline were all around. You can be fired from my airline for doing stupid things when you're traveling on an employee pass—like giving full vent to your anger in front of passengers.

So I kept my full venting to myself and later calmly explained to Tom a semiventing of my ideas on how this problem could be avoided in the future. Tom avoided strife by apologizing for leaving me and then calmly explaining that his first priority was to get Mandy to the toilet, not to help me with the luggage.

Neither one of us gave full vent to our anger. Which brings me to the second proverb for today: Proverbs 20:3, "It is to a man's honor to avoid strife, but every fool is quick to quarrel." Tom is the most honorable man I know when it comes to avoiding strife. He has a hothead for a wife, yet he manages to not act like a fool when I do. And he teaches me there is honor in this.

I suppose that's how to tell a wise man from a fool in two easy lessons. If you are wise (when you get angry), you don't give full vent to your anger. And if you are wise, you avoid strife.

Now, one last word of encouragement: What if you've been a fool your whole life—can you change? Yes, change is possible for everyone. Get a Bible and turn to Proverbs chapter 2. Do everything it says, and its promises will be yours. I know this because I used to give full vent to my anger and look at me now—I only semivent.

HUMILITY COMES
BEFORE HONOR

Humility comes before honor. Most people have to work at athletics or playing the piano or sculpting or anything that is honorable. People forget this and want honor the minute they set out to do something. But there is a learning curve.

One of the easiest places to forget there is a learning curve is in the process of writing. Most people think they should just sit down and be able to write. Like vomiting words. But writing is an art. And like most things in life, writing takes a lot of effort to make it look like it took no effort at all.

So, if you have been working seventeen years as I have on the first sentence of one novel, take heart. Honor is out there. It's just that the humble part of practice comes first.

TEN THINGS TO LOOK
FOR IN A HUSBAND

Sometimes I'm asked by people (especially those who know my mom was married five times) how I came to know what to look for in a husband the first time out. The answer to that is I spent ten years in a wonderful church where I watched healthy marriages at work. And I learned in those ten years what I needed to look for in a spouse. So, if you grew up in a home where role models weren't the best, get yourself around some people who can be examples to you. And read this essay. It is the ten ways I knew my husband was right for me

1. *I watched how his father treated his mother.* A man will almost always treat his wife the way his father treated his mother. I had a girlfriend once who I met while she was in the throes of a messy divorce, and I asked her how her husband's father had treated his mother. "Oh, terrible," she said, "but he realized that wasn't a good example." He

may have realized it, but he probably never spent much time around a model of healthy behavior, because he emulated the behavior he grew up with. Tom's father treated his mother with the respect of a man who realizes the value of a good wife. And he helped with dishes. These are important factors.

2. *Tom and I share a common faith and a common value system for determining that faith.* We both believe the Bible is a great guidebook to life itself.

3. *He laughs at my jokes.* It's very important that your spouse not just laugh at your silliness but laugh with you. Share a common sense of humor. And, of course, I think Tom is hilarious as well, the king of one-liners.

4. *He challenges my thinking.* If your spouse doesn't challenge your thinking before you are married, he will bore you spitless after marriage.

5. *He handles my weirdness.* Once I asked my husband if he knew how nuts I was before he married me. And he said, "Honey, that's why I married you." (Now, calm down from saying ahhhh and move on.) It's good if someone can handle, with ease, your weirdness. Sometimes on a walk with my husband, I'll be in a silly mood and start barking. Tom will calmly, without even looking over at me, say, "No barking." And I'll stop. He just understands and deals with my need to push the envelope.

6. *He is not an angry man.* The Bible gives numerous warnings about teaming up with an angry man. It's trouble. I think a great deal of anger comes with how we were treated as children by our parents. My husband was treated well by parents who loved each other. He is not an angry man.

7. *He has interests outside of me.* It's critical that whoever you marry has interests outside of you. Interests other than job interests. My husband likes to climb mountains and ride motorcycles. Yes, he shares my interest in good books, the arts, and long walks, but a good marriage of two people with common values is made interesting if both people have separate interests as well.

8. *He is patient.* I tested my husband's patience almost as soon as I met him. I can't remember what I said, but it was intended to push him, to see how he responded. I wanted to eliminate him as a candidate if he responded by being impatient or rude.

9. *He is gentle.* One of the attributes of God is his gentleness. My husband is like that, and it's attractive. This is an especially important quality if you plan to have children.

10. *He is kind.* Kindness makes a man attractive. My husband is the most attractive man I know.

INSIDE IMAGE

What you put into your heart, mind, and soul will determine the image that is reflected out.

INTUITION

D ivine intuition comes from God. The Bible says to "test the spirits." Sometimes we'll get a feeling of fear that we mistake for intuition. But perfect love casts out fear. God has not given us a spirit of fear. So, when we think we're being intuitive, we have to determine if that intuitiveness is divine or from something based in fear.

JESUS AS A SWEARWORD

Throughout the world, the name of Jesus is used as a swearword. I cannot understand how this came to be and why it hasn't changed in two thousand years. It must have to do with the power in the name. I do know that nothing causes passions to fly with more swiftness than just mentioning the name of Jesus at some gathering where people think the name doesn't apply to them. Even if I didn't believe in God, I'd have to be struck by the power of that name and the impact of a person who lived two thousand years ago, with no army and no great political power, who causes passion to ignite still today.

A CONTAINER FOR JOY

In God's presence is the fullness of joy. We come to him each morning, right where we are. We turn our hearts to be still and know him, reading the Bible, praying, seeking his will for our day. And then in the still of our encounters with God, we lift up our souls to be filled and we walk away, splashing joy as if we had a never-ending supply of it.

To you, O LORD, I lift up my soul.
—PSALM 25:1

THE JOYFUL FANATIC

The thing about being a Christian that is most compelling is the joy. Before I was following Christ, I didn't know joy like this was available. I knew happiness and I thought that was as good as it got. I also knew I was at war with God and had no idea it was possible to be at peace with him. I suppose if I'd known one could actually be at peace with God, I would have thought something like joy would be a result of it. But in the beginning I just didn't know.

Once I found out, I wanted to shake people and make them listen. It was for their own good. I've never been very good at keeping news to myself. And I wasn't a very calm Christian in the beginning. I yelled at people about the good news. It was the most exciting news I'd ever heard. I wanted to force everyone to God. It took me a long time to learn that people don't want to be yelled at or preached at. They like going their own way, and even if they didn't, they don't want some religious fanatic talking to them about being born again, for God's sake.

JUST AS I AM

That's how you come to Jesus: just as you are. Right where you are. Maybe you're in a brothel or an executive suite. Maybe you're on an airplane with your girlfriend, and your wife is at home. Maybe you're a depressed mother of a new baby. Just as you are, right where you are. That's how you come to Jesus. Then you find others just like you and you link arms and walk forward.

JOURNALING

A method of understanding who we are. The same can be said for our prayers.

JUDGING OTHERS

O ne of the reasons God tells us not to judge others is because it brings condemnation on ourselves. His laws are always in our best interest.

Judge not, and you shall not be judged.
—LUKE 6:37 (NKJV)

ACTING JUSTLY IS
A SCARY THING

I'm trying to teach our daughter what to do if she sees
some child being treated rudely or if she sees some
child being made fun of.

"Mandy," I tell her, "I would want you to speak
out. To say, 'Hey, stop that. That's not right.'"

"But, Mom," Mandy says, "what if they start making fun of me, too?"

I didn't tell Mandy this, but that is the argument of
every coward. Doing justly is a scary thing. In Nazi Ger-
many, it would cost you your life to stand up for a Jew.
In America before the Civil War, and long thereafter, it
might cost you your life to speak out on behalf of equal
rights for those whose color had long made them
oppressed. In some churches today, speaking up for
"dressing so our service will make the poor feel welcome"

could be met with loud ridicule. Doing what is just can be a scary thing.

And what does the LORD require of you?
To act justly and to love mercy
and to walk humbly with your God?
—MICAH 6:8

KNOWING GOD

B e still, and know that I am God" (Psalm 46:10). I
hate this command. And I love it. I hate it because
being still is the hardest thing I know how to do. I love
it because anyone can do it. Anyone can be still. Even
in the midst of chaos, we can take a moment deep
inside ourselves and say, *God, I want to seek you.* "And
the Word became flesh and made his dwelling among
us." *Lord, I want to seek your Word.* "In the beginning
was the Word, and the Word was with God, and the
Word was God." *God, I want to know your Word. I want
to be still and know you.*

That's how to know God: by being still before him,
not by blabbing on and on.

So, I'm going to stop right now and take some time
out of my day. Time out when I need to check e-mail
and return phone calls, when I need to clean toilets
because we're having guests for dinner tomorrow, when
I need to sew the curtains that have been lying on the
floor for months, when I need to hang up clothes and

do laundry. I'm going to stop everything and take time to sit down and be still and know God.

I'm going to be still and know, because if I'm not still before God, how will I get from the great Gift Giver the gift I'm supposed to be carrying around today? Perhaps it will be a gift of words. But I will only be gifted by spending time with the Giver of all good things.

THE LAST WEEK IS
THE HARDEST

I don't know why this is, but it is a truism. The last week of school, the last week of training, the last week before you leave to go on to a new job, the last week before the book is due, or the last week before your wedding date. The last week is the hardest. I'm in the last week right now, three days before my book is due, and I want to run away. I want to say, "You know it was all a mistake. I don't think I want to turn in a book like this to you." I'm looking for any excuse. Any excuse not to finish. I need to dust the corners of my house, the corners that can only be reached by a cotton-tipped swab. And because of that, well, you know, I can't possibly work on this final draft. The last week. Somehow it helps to remind myself it's always the most difficult. They say it will be like that just before Christ returns as well. The last days will be the most difficult.

LAUGHING AT YOURSELF

I've read Winnie-the-Pooh stories, but I'd never known anyone who had a personality just like Eeyore until I met Marlene. She amazes me with her ability to see disaster or a dark cloud behind every possible moment in life. Here are actual conversations I've had with Marlene over the years:

(1987) "I'm getting married, Marlene."

"Well, you know it's not all it's cracked up to be."

(1996) "We're going to have a baby, Marlene."

"Well, your life is over."

(2002) "We're getting a pool, Marlene."

"Oh, dear God, someone will drown for sure."

Once, after a particularly grueling fifteen minutes of talking to Marlene, in which she had found something negative to say about one hundred issues I'd run through, I stopped and said to her, "Marlene, at least in heaven everything will be good."

"What?" she said.

"Heaven," I said. "At least in heaven everything will be perfect."

Marlene paused as if thinking and then she said, "Sure. In the beginning."

Now, my pet peeve is negativity. I am convinced Marlene has some kind of a genetic predisposition to see the dark in this world where others see light. So what is it about her that makes me appreciate her as a friend? I'll tell you. It's because she can laugh at herself. There is a great deal to be said for someone who can laugh at herself.

For the thirty years I've known Marlene, I have played back her conversations for her, and she has, without exception, been able to see the humor in them. She can't change. She's been trying to be more positive for the entire time I've known her. Her efforts to be positive are even funnier because she will say something positive with a negative twist: "The sun is shining today. It's the first sun we've seen in days," or, "Sure, our sons are on the honor roll, but that just means an expensive college education."

But Marlene also has the ability to laugh at herself. There is humility in the ability to laugh at yourself. Laughing at yourself can be an acquired art. It takes practice. It involves not taking yourself too seriously. Try it. Even if you are just like Marlene, without the humor part. Try it. You'll be shocked at the good it will do you.

LEARNING

L ook at the football players in America as they practice. How do they get better at their sport? By con-
stantly running into huge obstructions. It's no different
in life. That's how we learn. It's how we get better.

*Consider it pure joy...whenever you
face trials of many kinds.*
—JAMES 1:2

THE LESSON OF THE
FUSSY HOUSEKEEPER
(FROM THE STORY OF
MARTHA AND MARY)

This is how I see Martha and Mary. Martha was the type of housekeeper whose home was always ready to receive visitors. She never had to—as I have had to—not let someone into her home because there was so much clutter on the floor she was mortified. On the other hand, Mary was a writer/thinker/artist type—as I am. She focused on what was aesthetically interesting to the point where she didn't see clutter or mess or even the need to help the hostess because she was so fixated on the one who had captivated her. Now, which one did Jesus praise, I ask you? So, my point: Don't ever show up at my home unexpectedly and hope to be let in.

Also, this type of person—the Mary type—can only

be happy in a marriage if she is married to someone like the man I married, who told me before we were married that if he wanted a housekeeper he'd hire one. (He must have meant that metaphorically because he's never shown interest in hiring a housekeeper.) Rather, he said, what he wanted was an interesting woman for a wife. I think he figured I at least knew the basics of cleaning. (Oh dear, the surprises we all find out after marriage.)

Now this whole argument breaks down when you find a woman who is an interesting woman *and* a fine housekeeper. I've known at least one of those in my lifetime. But I suspect my daughter will grow up like me: far more interested in reading a good book than in dusting. And I'm just trying to say, that isn't necessarily such a bad thing.

(For more on this read Luke 10:38-42.)

IT'S BETTER TO BE
LONELY SINGLE THAN
LONELY MARRIED

She was nineteen years old, the younger sister of a girlfriend who lived with me. And she was so anxious to get married. She didn't want to end up old and lonely like her twenty-seven-year-old spinster sister and me, the twenty-nine-year-old old maid. She wanted to be married. And she'd met such a cute guy. He loved to take her out and show her off. He wasn't the same faith, didn't have the same value system, but he liked to party and so did she.

The plans for the wedding were huge and consuming. Then the wedding was over and three months later she was in our apartment. "He doesn't like to spend nights at home," she said. "He wants to go out with his buddies."

Then she said, "I got married so I wouldn't be lonely,

and I'm lonelier married than I ever was single. At least when you're single there is some hope."

Her words haunted me, even though I didn't understand them until years later. I couldn't fathom how someone could be married and lonely, but I understand it now. Now I realize that it isn't the institution of marriage that takes away the loneliness; it's the relationship with your spouse that takes it away.

I used to ask my friend Janie if she liked being married, and she would say, "I like being married to Alan." That's another thing I never understood until I got married. *Who* you marry makes the difference between a commitment to joy and a commitment to sorrow.

THE LOST CHILD

In the days before I called 911 to report my daughter
had been kidnapped there had been numerous re-
ports on the national news about children who had
been taken from their homes. Just the night before I had
gone for a walk with my husband and asked him,
"What kind of person takes a child, steals a child away?"

"A sick, sick person," my husband said. So, the
whole kidnapping thing was in the front of my mind,
and I had made a mental note that if it happened to us,
I'd handle it with a calmness that comes to me in times
of crisis.

I was wrong about how I'd handle it. Yesterday,
when I dialed 911 to report our daughter was missing
from our home where she had been just five minutes
before, I wasn't calm. I wasn't composed. I was frantic.
Rational thought was out of the question.

Mandy had been playing in the big sand pile in our
backyard. We didn't have our fence up yet. She's five
years old and I'd left her for a few minutes to run back

into the house. I ran upstairs, got distracted, and it was a full five or ten minutes before I got back downstairs. I looked out at the sand pile and saw her toys and the imprint of where she had been sitting. She wasn't anywhere around. It looked as if someone had just lifted her out of the sand. I looked around the yard and at the forest bordering our property and at the lake, not a hundred yards from our house. Mandy wasn't anywhere. I ran back inside the house, checking every room, calling for her. She could have heard me from any room in the house. But the house was silent except for the hum of the air conditioner and the sound of our new outside water sprinklers.

I ran outside again and inside again. I hit every room again, yelling and knowing that my yelling wasn't doing any good. Outside again, I ran to all our neighbors, calling 911 on our cell phone. Most of the neighbors weren't home. When 911 answered, I yelled, "You've got to help me. My daughter is missing, someone has taken her. She was just here five minutes ago. " I was crying so hard they could barely understand me. When they asked me how old she was, I told them the wrong age. And I couldn't remember what she was wearing.

Two neighbors who were home came to help me look. I'd lost all hope. Mandy had been taken, and I was beyond devastated. *Oh God,* I prayed, sobbing, *Help me. Help me.* And as clear as any thought has ever come to me came the thought to go back in the house to the small shower in the master bedroom, the shower that is deeply recessed into the wall. You'd have to open the door to tell if anyone is in there and you can never hear that shower running.

It didn't make sense. Mandy has never taken a shower by herself. Never. And why would she start now—especially in that back shower, where you couldn't see in or out and couldn't hear a thing? It didn't make sense, but that's where she was.

She was proud of herself. "I got all sandy," she said. "So I took a shower all by myself. I had water running on my head and everything."

The police arrived as I was calling back 911 to tell them I'd found Mandy. They got out of the car and asked me where I'd found her. A strong urge came over me to tell them it was a miracle, that right after I'd called, I was able to nab the kidnapper and wrestle him to the ground and get a confession out of him while rescuing my daughter. Instead, I told them she was in the shower. I was mortified.

Later, while I was rocking Mandy in our rocking chair before she went to bed, I thought about God. He came to seek and to save the lost. I have a new vision of the heart of God. I have a new sense of what it feels like to have a child lost and to be devastated while frantically trying to find her and return her home.

In the same way your Father in heaven is not willing that any of these little ones should be lost.
—Matthew 18:14

LUST

In an odd sense, the greatest lust I have known and have observed is that of an infertile mother for a baby. Women who have struggled with infertility for a while cannot look at other mothers who have babies; it causes them pain. They can't go to church on Mother's Day. They can't eat or think or sleep without the thought of wanting that baby. They go to the doctor, who tells them a completely wrong answer. "Go home and forget about it," he says. That's ridiculous. What they need to do is what anyone with any lust needs to do to escape its hold on their life: They need to fill that place where the lust exists with something else. Something they love with the same passion as the thing they lusted after. And something good.

For example, many infertile couples suddenly become pregnant when they adopt a child or even get a pet. This is because they have poured something wonderful into that hole in their life. I saw the truth of this when I finally—after eight years of infertility—got pregnant. I had been kicked out of the infertility program due to my age. Then I got involved with a writing project. I literally fell in love with my work; it became my passion. A few weeks later, I discovered I was pregnant.

Lusting after something drains you. Filling that drain with something good sets you free and gets you beyond your loss.

THE MARRIAGE BED

The Bible says the marriage bed is undefiled and what goes on there is undefiled. This is a pure mystery of God.

THE MOST IMPORTANT
THING TO LOOK FOR IN
A MARRIAGE PARTNER

This may sound odd, but the most important thing to look for in a marriage partner is a common value system. I told this to a flight attendant once, and she said, "*Oh, I know that's true!* When my husband and I went shopping for the first time before we were married, he picked out the same kind of toothpaste and soap…and I knew he was the one!"

What I'm talking about here is a value system more complex than choices of toothpaste and soap. If you have a common value system and nothing else, your marriage can thrive, like the marriages that have been arranged. Even if you have everything else going for you—riches and physical attraction and mental stimulation and common interests—if you don't have a common value system, the marriage will be difficult, more difficult than it has to be.

This is why Paul tells us not to be unequally yoked. The more passionate you are about your values, the more frustrated you will be when someone you are bound to doesn't share those values.

HOW TO GROW
A MIRACLE

To grow a miracle, you start with a problem. The bigger the seed of the problem, the better potential it has for miracle growth. You begin by praying over that seed. If it's a firmly planted problem, all the better. If it's planted out where everyone can see it, better still. As you pray, you water the problem with tears, and then in the light of God's Word a miracle blooms.

Almost all miracles begin as problems—it's just one of the mysteries of God. Sometimes the only miracle is a change in our attitude toward the problem.

THE MOST
COMMON MISTAKE

The most common mistake is not admitting you make mistakes on a daily basis. And that your mistakes are just as bad as anyone you know. We are all in desperate need of help.

For all have sinned and fall
short of the glory of God.
—ROMANS 3:23

MOURNING WHAT IS LOST

M andy's bunny died last week. And Mandy is crying about it. And talking about all that bunny meant to her. And her reaction is healthy. That's what to do when your bunny dies. Cry. And talk about it. Mourn the loss. If you don't mourn the loss of your bunny and release it, you won't be prepared to handle the loss of greater things in life.

Because a great deal of life contains loss. The loss of our dreams. The loss of a date who chose someone else. The loss of our heroes. The loss of our pets and of relatives. The loss of our career. Learning to lose, mourning the loss and releasing it, prepares us to go on.

If we don't mourn losses and release them, we are stuck, unable to move ever again. And things that don't move stagnate.

There is...a time to mourn.
—ECCLESIASTES 3:1,4

WHEN NO IS
AN ANSWER

Sometimes the quickest way to a yes is to take no for an answer. Think about it. God hears no as an answer from most of us every day. Yet he is patiently waiting for a yes. My prayer is to be more patient, like God, and not force a yes when someone says no.

OLD FURNITURE

I love the book *A Severe Mercy* by the late Sheldon Vanauken. In that book, Vanauken describes how he and the love of his life purchased a car and immediately took a sledgehammer to it so they wouldn't be captivated by the overimportance of a *thing*.

I'm not to that point yet. But my husband and I do furnish our home with things we can allow someone to ruin without too much pain. At least, we always did do that until we recently decided to get a leather couch—the first leather furniture we've owned in fifteen years of marriage. It lasted only a few months in our living room and then had to be replaced with a more durable tapestry couch that would allow me to love the neighborhood children instead of secretly seething at them when they approached our couch feet first.

I want to remember that people are more important than things. The importance of this lesson is brought home to me when I visit someone's home where I fear that my five-year-old will knock off some crystal thing they value so much and that their sorrow over that thing would exceed their love for my daughter.

A PARENT'S LOVE

I was completely unprepared for how consuming it is to become a parent. People had warned me it was like having another job. What a joke! It wasn't like any job I'd ever had. There's no other job where you're on duty twenty-four hours a day, seven days a week, while dying of sleep deprivation for *years* at a time. And I was unprepared for the fact that even when you aren't with the baby, she consumes your thoughts.

Mandy is five years old now, and I'm starting to adjust to having another person depend on me for all her food, clothes, training, entertainment, medical well-being, and everything else she needs. And I've finally accepted the fact that she has expanded my brain with thoughts of her, day and night. Even dreams of her.

This whole experience has made me understand why God uses references to being our parent in Scripture. It is the closest caring relationship there is, and he's trying to let us know how he feels about us and how dependent he would like us to be on him.

As a father has compassion
on his children,
so the LORD has compassion
on those who fear him.
—PSALM 103:13

PERSPECTIVE

When we view the world from our perspective, we are like a bunch of ants trying to view the universe from their perspective. Even if you had some wise ants, if they lean on their own understanding or their own perspective, they will be limited by the dimensions of size.

That's why God doesn't want us to lean on our own understanding. Our understanding is born out of our perspective, which is too limited to do us overall good.

Trust in the LORD with all your heart
and lean not on your own understanding.
—Proverbs 3:5

PINCHING PEOPLE
TO JESUS

I used to think you could *make* people come to Jesus. My approach to evangelism was to tell people they needed to come to Jesus and if they said no, I pinched them. This "come to Jesus or I'll kill you" method was most evident in my first target: my brother Joe.

When I was nine and Joe was eight, I was big for my age and he was little for his. Thus, he did whatever I told him. But usually he put up some kind of a verbal fight. (Years later, in college, he would become a national debate champion—a skill he honed with me.)

When I first heard the good news of God sending his Son to die for our sins, I wanted everyone to "get saved." And my plan was to start with Joe. So, I made him come to church with me and I allowed him to sit through one entire sermon without pressuring him to respond. He didn't respond, so that evening in our little church in northwest Washington State I told him either he went forward to become a Christian or he'd be sorry. And I pinched him, for good measure.

He looked right at me and said, "No."

"Yes," I said.

"No," he said. (His debating skills weren't perfected yet.)

"Yes," I said, and pinched him again. "Go!" I said. The congregation was singing the second verse, and we didn't have a lot of time. *"Go!"* I said again.

"No!" he said. This went on for one full minute. Finally, twenty-three pinches later, each one more painful than the last, my brother went forward. I went with him, pinching him all the way down the aisle.

The minister looked at my brother and saw what he assumed to be the fear of God in his eyes. "Do you want to receive Jesus?" he said.

"Yes, he does," I said.

And right there the minister had my brother repeat a simple prayer, which I took to be success. I had succeeded where the Holy Spirit had failed. I'd forced my brother into the kingdom of God.

Years later my brother told me he hadn't really received Jesus that day.

"But you went forward!" I said, wondering if I should start pinching him again.

"Change doesn't come by going through the motions. It has to come from inside," he said. "It's a personal choice. God gave us free will."

As I've grown up in my faith, one of the most shocking things I've learned about evangelism is that

Jesus never pinched anyone into the kingdom. If someone came to him, they did it freely, and if they didn't come, he left them in their choices—choices with eternal consequences, but still he honored people by allowing them to say no.

I want to be more like that. I want to love people so much that when they say no, I respect their answer as their choice. I can still go off alone and pray for them in secret. But I don't want to pinch anybody to Jesus because I want to be like him, and the Bible says, "God's kindness leads you toward repentance" (Romans 2:4).

PLEASING GOD

Hebrews 11:6 says there are two ways to please God. First, you must believe that he is, and second, you must believe that he is a rewarder of those who diligently seek him. I find it interesting that God places such an importance on our belief in his reward system. Like a good coach who says after this exercise there will be free ice cream all around or a teacher who says if you graduate with honors you'll be flown to Disneyland. Somehow God wants to convey to us that he, too, is into rewards. Those who diligently seek him will be rewarded. What kind of Creator of the universe is this, who holds the universe in one hand and rewards for those who diligently seek him in the other?

PLEASURE

One of the reasons I follow God is for the sheer joy of it, for the pleasure of it both now and to come. The best analogy I have for this in the natural world is a runner training to run a race. The training involves focus and letting go of anything that is weighing you down. You don't mind letting go of the weights because you are so fixed on your goal. Then, as you run the race, the running itself is exhilarating. Adrenaline flows—a rush like nothing else—and at the end of the race, you have the joy of reaching your goal.

Psalm 16:11 is my favorite verse:

> You will show me the path of life;
> In Your presence is fullness of joy;
> At Your right hand are pleasures
>   forevermore. (NKJV)

That verse, more than any other, defines why I am a Christian.

POSSESSIONS

Luke 12:15 says, "A man's life does not consist in the abundance of his possessions." I know of no other verse that goes so against modern advertising in the Western world. Modern advertising tells you, "He who dies with the most toys wins" and suggests that you will be more of a person if you drive a certain car or live in a certain area or wear a certain designer. What would happen if we spent one whole day contrasting the messages we receive from mass advertising with this verse? A man's life does not consist in the abundance of his possessions. It's a radical thought.

YOU CAN PRAY
ABOUT ANYTHING

Some people say you can't pray about what you weigh. I say you can pray about anything—no one can stop you.

Some people say you can't pray about the fact that you don't have any faith. They say, "What if God finds out what you are thinking and says, 'I'm *shocked!* Those thoughts are stinking!'"

I say God knew the stink of your think a long time ago and just to show the weight of your worth, he sent his Son to this low earth.

Some people say you can't pray about hating your neighbor.

I say if you can't pray about what ails you, why is God called the Great Physician? And why are we told to cast all our care on him? He's big enough to handle it. He said pray about everything.

But some people say you can't pray in school, because what if the school board finds out you're disrupting the peace?

I say you can pray about anything. They can't read your mind, and God says pray all the time.

So, wherever you are and whatever you do, pray about it, pray about it—no one can stop you.

A Twelve-Word
Prayer

L ord, let me be a fool for no sake other than yours."

PRAYER IS STRONGER
THAN MAGIC

Magic is defined as something that "invokes the supernatural." C. S. Lewis once referred to Christianity as a kind of white magic. We all know there is a black magic. Go with me for a minute here and use the analogy of Christianity being a kind of white magic. If that were true, then the wand God has given his subjects to wave is prayer. It is a wand that invokes the supernatural. We are told to pray without ceasing. Why? Because we are healed as we pray. And we heal others with our prayers. But that's where the analogy breaks down: Prayer is more powerful than magic. Whoever heard of a wand of such magic it healed both the one using it and the one for whom it is used?

The wand of prayer: Some of us use it freely, but

some of us put it on the floor and forget about it, not
rendering it powerless, just choosing to ignore the gift
of its power in our lives.

The earnest prayer of a righteous person has
great power and wonderful results.
—JAMES 5:16, NLT

PRIDE

If we say we do not struggle with pride, it is probably because we have given into the temptation. The struggle itself is a sign of a healthy attitude.

IN PRISON
WITH GRANDMA

S he doesn't want me to use her real name, so I'll just call her Joy. That's what she reminds me of: joy. Grandma Joy, she would prefer. She is somewhere past the age of sixty, and her white hair frames her face, reflecting light like a halo. She's very peppy and something about her doesn't seem to fit with the job she's chosen for herself. She is a lay minister to the kids at the county detention center.

I won't say what town; she doesn't want me to reveal that either. "The wounds are too fresh," she says. "My son wouldn't understand."

But I had to ask her about it. "How did you come by this job, Grandma Joy? Something about you and detention doesn't fit."

"We were living life here in the Midwest, raising our children, when my youngest got involved with drugs. He went off to California and got himself arrested." Her voice starts to shake. She won't look at me, when she comes to this part of the story. "We were so far away and had the farm here and the expense was so great… The whole time he was in there, the whole two years, we were only able to visit him once. At that time I just thought how wonderful it would be if there was one mother out there in California who would visit my son and be a mother to him when I couldn't be there—who would love on him in my stead. And shortly after that, I determined that I would be that mother here, in my hometown. I would visit kids here and love them as if they were my own."

And so she does. At first she'd had to learn the system. She didn't want to just visit the kids in the detention center because they are only allowed so many visitors and she didn't want to have her visits count against them in case their relatives showed up. So, she went to her church and found out she could become a "lay clergy."

"Any church can designate a lay clergy," she tells me. And clergy visits don't count against the kids. Then she got some materials to teach a little Bible class and that became her focal point. Three nights a week she's at the detention center teaching the incarcerated kids about a God who loves them and knew all about their future mistakes when he sent his Son as a demonstration of his love. "And as further proof of his love, he sent me," she says, with a hug to each kid.

Grandma Joy asked me to come and speak to her kids—the ones locked up for crimes against society. I did, and on the way home in the car with Grandma Joy, I commented about the irony of her pain becoming another mother's gain.

"God needs people experienced in pain," she said. "It's we who are experienced in pain who get the greatest audience."

Someday when we get to heaven, you will know Grandma Joy's real name, but until then, join me in contemplating her response to the pain of a child gone astray. And ponder with me for a minute her words, "God needs people experienced in pain."

THE BENEFIT
OF KEEPING QUIET

S ometimes just by keeping your mouth shut you will be thought wise. (This is a paraphrase of Proverbs 17:28.)

Of course, I know nothing of this by personal experience, but I have seen it in others.

IT'S NOT REJECTION;
IT'S REDIRECTION

I f you are able to look at rejection not as a negative but a positive, it helps. For example, the next time someone turns you down for a job, you say, "Well, thank God for that, because it's obviously not where I was supposed to be."

Of course, this viewpoint only works if you believe God is guiding your steps. If you don't, it will be more difficult. But, as someone who believes in God, it has helped me greatly when I send out an idea for publication and some evil person rejects it. Then I can say, *Every closed door means I must turn and try another. How else could God guide me but through slammed doors?* Now, if doors continue to slam, as in the case of one of the writing projects currently on my desk, then I say, "Well, this must mean wait." Sometimes rejection is God's way of saying, "Wait." But most of the time it's God's way of saying, "Try another door."

WHAT TO DO
WHEN YOU MURDER
YOUR REPUTATION

I t was not my idea to put the dead bunny in the freezer. I wanted to leave it in the trash where my husband had placed it (all wrapped in plastic) after he'd discovered it with its feet pointing to heaven.

But our daughter overheard her daddy talking to me on the phone, telling me her ex-pet was now "safely in the garage." So she went to look for it. When she couldn't find it, she began hurling questions at her dad as to "exactly where in the garage" he put that bunny. She wanted a funeral, she said. She wanted a proper burial. Tom got tired of dodging questions, so last night he crept outside, dug through the trash, and retrieved the plastic-wrapped bunny. Then he put it in the freezer.

I was horrified. So horrified that I asked a friend to please set the record straight—should my whole family be wiped out tonight—as to why this author, who writes about God, was found to be storing in her freezer a rabbit that had obviously been dead for days.

I'm extra sensitive over this whole thing because I think it was I who killed the bunny. The night before we got little Fluffy, I installed six high-frequency electrical plugs all over our house to get rid of any mice we might have. The plugs were guaranteed to keep rodents away. I didn't think of a bunny as a rodent when his cage got placed within three feet of the sound-emitting devices.

My husband doesn't think it was the frequency plugs that killed the bunny; he thinks the bunny died of bunny diarrhea brought on by the wrong food. But, either way, I'm thinking what we need to do now is get Fluffy off ice and into a proper burial.

I'm writing about this today because while Daddy was home with Mandy, the Saturday her bunny died, Mommy was at a writers conference killing something else: my reputation. And once again, it wasn't that I meant to kill this most important thing, it was an accident.

I was on drugs. I normally never take drugs stronger than aspirin, but right before the conference I'd experienced my first-ever strained back and the doctor had prescribed cortisone.

It turns out I could have played football while on cortisone. I became exceedingly aggressive and completely unaware it was me with the aggression problem. All of a sudden the entire population at the writers conference I was attending seemed like idiots, and it was clearly my duty to point this out—to everyone. For example, when one of 450 attendees who hadn't read my first book implied that, as a flight attendant/author, I might not have anything to say, I reached across the dinner table so my face was close to hers and hissed, "Don't have anything to say? I have plenty of things to say!"

When I finished with her, everyone at the table was stunned into silence except one woman who boldly mentioned that I needed to learn how to deal with people. I also hissed at her. And I couldn't understand it when no one seemed to talk to me the rest of the meal.

It was as if I'd turned into a fire-breathing dragon at the conference center. As I sat next to an award-winning author and slaughtered my reputation before his eyes, I could not understand why the rest of the table was staring at me with such disgust and horror—until two days later when the effects of the cortisone wore off, and I realized what I'd done.

So, what do you do when you've killed your daughter's bunny and murdered your reputation? Well, after a cooling-off period, you give the dead a proper burial. I contacted the one person I knew at that table and asked his forgiveness. The others are out there somewhere, complete strangers. If they are reading this book: I didn't mean it—I was on drugs.

But, I am thinking, there's not a lot you can do right away to fix something like a murdered reputation or a dead rabbit. You do what you can and move on, having learned a thing or two. And that's exactly what I, ex-bunny-killer and all, intend to do.

HOW TO BE A SAINT

M y definition of a saint is someone who offers to
baby-sit for people with small children once a
week, on Friday nights, from 6 to 11 P.M.

If there were a saint like this in my life, I would call
her the matron-saint-of-our-family-of-serious-baby-
sitting, and she would be revered and pictures of her
would appear in the most hallowed of places, stuck with
magnets onto our refrigerator door. If you are a person
who wonders how God could use you, then offer your
services to a family for free, even once a month. God
will bless you for it. And I will call you a saint.

SEEKING

Jesus said to "seek first the kingdom of God." The times I have, I have been so full of joy I cannot contain it, and the times I haven't, I have blamed my lack of joy on the source of joy himself.

THE SELF-MADE MAN

When someone says he is self-made or implies he has pulled himself up to greatness, he reminds me of my five-year-old saying she is a self-made woman.

Mandy forgets it is her father and I who supply her home and clothes and food. Self-made men forget it is God who supplies the air they breathe and the good health they enjoy, and it is God who instills in them the ability to succeed. Self-made men are like children who don't see the constant care of a Father behind the scenes.

SEX AND YOUR SOUL

Hollywood has it all wrong when they say that sex is free. That is like saying that fire is free. Fire is something you have to be careful not to mess around with. It is best used in a confined environment. If you take it out of a grill where you're using it to cook a great meal, you've got a problem. It will burn your house down.

Sex is like that: It was made to be used in the confines of marriage. In those confines it becomes a tool in the creation of a great marriage. But outside the confines of marriage, it will hurt your self-worth, scar your soul, and damage your spirit.

That's why those who have been sexually abused or sexually promiscuous are victims of scarred souls. But the incredible news is that our God is in the business of restoring souls that have been burned, scarred, charred. It may take him years. He may use lots of counselors and loads of time to make the process complete. But he does bring back a luster to souls.

"The LORD is my shepherd, I shall not be in want. He makes me lie down in green pastures, he leads me beside quiet waters, he *restores* my soul" (Psalm 23:1-3, emphasis added). Oh, Jesus, thank you.

Maybe your soul today is scarred by the fire you have played with or been burned by. Or maybe your soul has just never been polished with the soft cloth of God's love and so it's tarnished from years of neglect. Have you ever seen an old antique that has been restored by an expert? You couldn't even tell there was once any damage. The thing gleams and shines and becomes the most beautiful piece of furniture in the house.

When one has a soul restored by the greatest restorative master, it's the same way. That soul will become the most beautiful thing in the house.

WHY WE SING

The command to sing is one of the most repeated commands in the Bible. I think it's repeated so often because singing, even if it's just in the heart, has power to change reactions to circumstances. That's all most of us can change anyway. That's what our choice is and we always have a choice. How will you react? That's your choice. (Sometimes I hate it that I have a choice, because it makes me have to be responsible for my actions. But it's true.) You can choose how you are going to react. If you are singing to God, the choice leads down the road to joy.

THE SMALL BUSINESS
OF MARRIAGE

Somehow I expected marriage to be some type of elongated date. No matter how much people tried to tell me that wasn't true, I thought I knew better—in *our* marriage it would be true.

But now that we have been married fifteen years, I find that marriage is a lot like running a small business. Where will this money go? What bill will we pay? Is buying a new car more important than putting in a lawn? Do you really need that motorcycle? Do I really need to go to yet another writers conference? Things like these become the questions of the day. Not, "How do I love thee? Let me count the ways."

Of course, marriage isn't always like this. Sometimes, before children for instance, it's easier to have more romance. And even when it is like a small business, I have to say there are benefits to marriage, like someone to call when your day goes wrong. Or when it's gone right. My point is just that marriage isn't all roses and kisses. Sometimes it's killing the mouse that is eating its way through your Christmas ornaments while you're fighting over how much money you've spent on presents this year—while your daughter is crying because you won't let her have a horse.

SOLAR POWER

We have these lights in our front yard that are *solar powered*. The only way they shine in the dark is if they have sat in the light of the sun all day.

Sometimes when it's cloudy, they don't get sunlight. They still look the same on the outside, but the truth of their lack of power shows up at night, when they are no good for guiding anyone home.

TIME

How much time do you have to spend in God's Word in order to be blessed? Asking this question is like asking how much time do you have to spend being loved by someone you adore and who adores you to be blessed. Well, you only have to spend a minute, and if you want to be more blessed, you spend every minute.

As a rule for Bible meditation, I like to rely on the time sequence outlined in the second chapter of Proverbs. Proverbs 2 starts out by saying to seek the Word and wisdom of the Word. Proverbs 2:4 says to look for it as silver and search for it as hidden treasure. Most people I know work eight hours a day, five days a week, seeking silver. I suppose those seeking hidden treasure work round the clock. So, I would suggest for starters you let the forty-hour week be your goal. But, "How?" you cry: "I work full time and have a family." Well, what you do is paste a Bible verse on your mirror and on your door and on your car dashboard. And on your desk at work and in your pocket, and you can write one on your thumbnail. I do that sometimes, with indelible ink, so it doesn't rub off. Just a short verse, so I can meditate on it while I'm bored. I'm not telling you what you have to do. I'm just telling you what works for me.

Proverbs 2 says if you do this, if you take God's Word seriously, then you will understand the fear of the Lord and find the knowledge of God. (Now, that's powerful.) It also says you will get wisdom, knowledge, and understanding. There will be victory in store for you, and God will be a shield to you. It says a few more things, too, like how you will begin to have discretion that will protect you and understanding that will guard you.

There are so many weirdos out there vying for your soul and your time that I pray you will have discretion as a shield and understanding as a guard. I pray you will take God's Word as seriously as you take the search for silver.

YOUR TRAGEDY IS
NOT YOUR IDENTITY

A close friend of mine has been through horrors in
life. But the problem is, she thinks of herself in
those terms: someone who has been through horror.
Right away, when you meet her, you will hear all about
her tragedy. Her tragedy has become her identity. It is
the filter through which she views herself.

I have another friend who has been successful in
Hollywood. Her success goes before her. People approach her and say, "Aren't you that actress? Didn't I see
you on TV? What happens now that the 'soap' has let
you go? What will you do now? Who will you be?"

I was thinking about both these women this week,
the one who chooses to view her identity through her
tragedy and the one whose identity is viewed by others
through the filter of her acting success. And I was thinking our identity isn't really found in our tragedy or our
success.

Well, then, for goodness' sake, where is it found? It is found for the sake of goodness, from the very center of goodness. In the work of whose we are.

We are God's workmanship, created in Christ Jesus for good works, which he has prepared in advance for us to do. How exciting is that! We have work to do, and it was all set out for us in a wonderful plan for our lives before we were even born. And we are the very workmanship of God.

I like to think of my identity that way, as the work of the ultimate designer, a designer whose work has been admired since the beginning of time—who planned goodness for me before I arrived on earth.

For we are God's workmanship.
—Ephesians 2:10

HOW TO BE UNIQUE

The surest way to be unique is to be innocent of evil. As innocent as you can possibly be. People will be drawn to you.

Goodness has innumerable facets—when someone is unique, there is always something more to discover.

Evil has only one side to it, and after a while, it is boring.

THERE WILL
ALWAYS BE THINGS
WE DON'T UNDERSTAND

M ark Twain said, "It's not the parts of the Bible I
don't understand that bother me, it's the parts I
do." I suggest we concentrate on the parts of the Bible
we understand. For example, what if I really loved my
enemies and prayed for those who are spiteful to me?
The effect of one person, obeying that one verse, could
be staggering.

THE VALENTINE'S
DAY GLOW

A ll I wanted for Valentine's Day 2002 was to get our
Christmas tree down and put away.

I know you're thinking: *I didn't read that correctly.
Christmas tree? They still had their Christmas tree up?*

Yes, we did.

And no, it was not intentional. Sometimes things
just get pushed to the back burner.

My daughter and I had been doing a lot of traveling.
My husband had been working twelve hours a day and
he was exhausted when he got home. Wrapping decora-
tions and taking down the three parts to the fake tree
and putting them in the attic just weren't a top priority.

I know people looked at our tree and my messy car
and said, "What is the deal with her?" So, it was interesting to me when I read a verse in the Bible that said of
Jesus, "There is no beauty or majesty in his appearance." How encouraging is that? There was no beauty

or majesty in Jesus' appearance. Nothing that would make people desire him. I mean, come on, the guy probably didn't have deodorant and I bet he didn't have a lot of choice in clothes and no coin-op laundry. Yet he had what I call the Valentine's Day Glow. It's the glow that comes from knowing you are loved by the one most important in your life.

Have you ever seen someone in love? It doesn't matter what else is going on, they just glow. There was a guy in the Bible named Stephen who had that glow. And Moses had it when he came down off the mountain. And apparently Jesus had it, because people were attracted to him. They followed him like metal will follow a magnet. And he offers it to us—this glow that attracts. Whoever will, may come and spend time with him. To fall in love with him. The Glow is a byproduct of time spent with the love of our life.

I've had that glow a few times. I always know when I've got it because later I realize that I didn't care a whit about how I looked; I cared only about sharing the joy of the love of the one who loves me. Who gives me that Valentine's glow.

In November 2001, I spoke at a college in Lincoln, Nebraska. I know I had the glow then because the night before I had tried to dye my hair…in spots. And it hadn't turned out. So, I had kind of a purple spot on top and some orange spots underneath and some gray spots under that. But I didn't care. I was so in love with Jesus, so immersed in his Word and the joy of sharing it, that I spoke at that college and had my purple-head picture taken for a large poster, not realizing until later how bad it looked. I didn't care about appearances then; I had that Valentine's Day Glow.

I pray this week that we will all take time to be with the lover of our soul. That we will fall so in love with him that nothing else will matter. Nothing—not purple-spotted hair or even the thought of a Christmas tree still standing, fully decorated, in the dining room.

VICTORY

He holds victory in store for the upright" (Proverbs 2:7). If I were not a Christian, this one verse would intrigue me greatly—because what if it's true?

VISION

Getting to know the Light of the World clarifies vision.

WAITING: THE STORY
OF MY LIFE

Sometimes my daughter cuddles up to me and says, "Tell me the story of your life." Then she leans in and burrows the top of her head till it's snug under my left arm. I look over at her and realize she's only five years old, so I have to tell her the story in just five minutes. This is the story I tell her.

Once upon a time there was a little girl who didn't have a nice stepfather, so mostly she stayed alone at the library and read books. She read lots of books and one of them was the Bible. In the Bible, she read about a God who answers prayers. So the little girl prayed to that God. She prayed three prayers. She wanted to be a writer someday. She wanted to have a wonderful family someday. And she wanted to be a blessing to others.

When she grew up and left the mean stepfather, she ran into a problem. She met a handsome man with a fast red car and lots of flashy money. The man didn't believe in God or anything he couldn't see. The girl was nineteen years old now, and she looked at the fancy car and the flashy money and decided to forget about God. She decided to marry the man and she told God that there was nothing he could do about it. She said, "God can't stop me."

But God did stop her. She was in an auto accident, and while she was in the hospital, she was humbled and told God she would seek him now. She started reading her Bible again and starting going to a Bible-teaching church.

For the next ten years the girl learned a lot about Jesus and she fell so in love with Jesus that she decided in her heart she would never marry anyone who wasn't God's choice for her.

God tested her decision, year after year, by allowing all her friends to get married until there was only her left. Then the girl wasn't young anymore and wasn't as pretty anymore, and she worried that the man God would provide for her might not be able to see or chew—but still she trusted God.

Years later, God brought a Prince Charming into the girl's life and he was the most wonderful thing and most handsome thing the girl could ever even imagine. And God blessed their marriage with a happiness the girl had never known. *Wait for the Lord.*

The happy couple wanted a baby. But God didn't give them one. For eight years they prayed and for eight years they trusted in modern medicine. Then the doctors said, "Nothing will work. It's impossible." But the girl believed in prayer, so she prayed for a miracle. One day, October 22, 1996, God provided that miracle, and the happy couple gave birth to a miracle baby called Amanda Joy. Miracle Mandy. God took a long time to answer that prayer too. *Wait for the Lord.*

Then in 2001, after thirty years of writing, God answered the last prayer of the little girl. She got a book published. And then last week, someone wrote to her and said, "Your book is a blessing to me. Your life is a blessing to me." And that's when the girl, who was now an old lady, with a young husband and a little girl of her own and a brand-new book that was a blessing, knew God had answered all the prayers of her childhood.

And for all her life in all her ways, that girl, who is your mommy, now says,

Wait for the Lord.

Wait for the LORD;
be strong and take heart
and wait for the Lord.
—Psalm 27:14

WHAT GOD CHOOSES

"God hath chosen the foolish things of the world to confound the wise" (1 Corinthians 1:27, KJV). He used Paul, the apostle who was a murderer of Christians, to become one of Christianity's most outspoken evangelists. He used Job, a very blessed man, to become the central character in a story about a man who seems to be cursed. He used a stall full of straw and animals to house the Savior of the world. And he used a simple flight attendant to write this book.

The next time you think God can't use you, think again. He's used some pretty unusual things.

WHAT YOU
DON'T KNOW
CAN HURT YOU

It had been a beautiful California summer day. The sun had shown bright and I'd driven over to visit my grandmother just as it was setting. Grandma lived in a not-that-great neighborhood, but in those days I didn't worry about crime. Crime seemed to be the type of thing that happened only to other people.

My grandma and I laughed, shared a meal, and talked. When I left her house, I was feeling as happy as I'd ever felt.

I got into my little VW bug and remembered that I'd left all the windows down to keep it cool. Opening the driver's side door, I didn't look in the back seat. Why would I?

Pulling out of the driveway and heading for the first intersection, I thought I heard someone move in the back seat. I decided it was my imagination until I felt his hand rest lightly on my shoulder. I froze in place. Couldn't say a word. Stunned. My worst fears realized. And I became more afraid when I began to feel his hot breath on the back of my neck.

I didn't know what to do so I continued driving, hoping I'd get to a populated place before he'd ask me to pull over. But I seemed to be so shaken with fear that despite myself, I started to slow down. Maybe I could stop and get out and run.

I didn't say anything and he didn't say anything; he just kept resting his hand on my shoulder. Or was it the edge of a gun? But it was warm through the shirt on my shoulder, not cold like steel. He was getting nervous, I could tell. His breathing seemed to be coming more quickly now.

Of course, I didn't know what was going to happen, but finally the suspense of him not saying anything, just keeping his hand there, and his breathing so fast, got to me. *What do you want?* I said in a loud voice and stopped the car. At that moment, the huge cat who had found refuge in my car and been poised for the window took his paw off my shoulder, screeched, and leaped out onto the pavement.

It was several minutes before I could start up the car again. First, I just sat there and laughed with relief. Then I looked in the back seat to make sure there was no one there and got out and rolled up all the windows of my little car. Then I cautiously continued on my way.

I'd been terrorized by what I thought was something awful, and it was a *cat's paw* and a *cat's breath*. I made a silent commitment to be more careful in the future.

Now, I think there is a spiritual lesson here. Just as I responded to something in the dark that seemed to be what it was not, there is something in our world that is what it doesn't seem to be.

The Bible says there are evil forces so sinister that we are actually in a struggle with them. A spiritual struggle. We may not see them. We may not recognize them for what they are. But they are there. And, the Bible says, there is a way to dress that will allow you to survive the battle. It's about wearing proper armor.

For our struggle is not against flesh and blood,
but against the rulers, against the authorities,
against the powers of this dark world
and against the spiritual forces of evil
in the heavenly realms.
Therefore put on the full armor of God.
—EPHESIANS 6:12-13

WHY THINGS
ALWAYS GO WRONG

Why do things always have to go wrong?" That was the cry of my neighbor as she sat on our back deck and we laughed about her fence problems and our pool problems.

My neighbors had decided to put up a fence. It was prefab. All they had to do was drill a few holes six feet apart for anchor posts. The first hole went in great. Holes two, three, and four cut the cable, the sprinklers, and the phone. That's when they stopped digging holes.

I smiled at their antics, thinking I was glad nothing like that was going to happen to us.

You see, we weren't the do-it-yourself kind of people. Then we bought a simple vinyl pool. All you had to do was fill the thing with water, and it was supposed to stand up by itself. The pool was fifteen feet across and almost four feet deep. The directions said to make sure the ground was clear and level before you set out the pool. We cleared and smoothed the ground. It wasn't completely level, but could a 5 percent slope really matter?

It turns out a 5 percent slope under a vinyl pool that holds thirty-one hundred gallons of water really matters. Within an hour of the pool's being filled, the heavy side of it began to lean. As the day wore on, that side leaned more until it began to crawl to a roll. Hours later, it was obvious the pool was going to tip over and wash away all our newly laid sod.

So, we decided to drain it and start over, only the plug in the pool didn't drain it fast enough, so we borrowed a sump pump to pump the water out. Nobody told us not to stand a sump pump upright in a vinyl pool because it'll cut a hole in the bottom of the pool. Four holes later, we'd figured that out.

We patched the holes, waiting hours for them to dry.

The next day, my husband went to work releveling the ground. He worked for hours with a two-by-four and a level until he cleared an entire circle exactly fifteen feet in diameter. But when he set the pool up, one side of it didn't get in the circle. Instead it went onto the two-inch ledge surrounding the circle, and two thousand gallons later he realized he had another big problem. That's when he drained the pool, kicked the tree, and had a forty-five-minute sit on our back deck alone with his head in his hands.

The pool is now piled in our garage, and I've been thinking about my neighbor's question, "Why do things always have to go wrong?"

There are two answers to why things always have to go wrong. First, things go wrong because things are not right on this earth. Somewhere deep in our soul we know this, no matter what we believe. If things were perfect on earth, we'd never long for more.

The second reason things go wrong is to give us a chance to grow in grace and show that grace to others. People grow by coming up against tests and passing them. It's true in athletics, it's true in math class, and it's true in our walk with God.

So, the next time something goes wrong, consider it a joy, a chance to grow—and remind me of this the next time you see me, will you?

WISDOM

I f I could just get one thing across in this book, it would be to read the wisdom of Solomon as recorded in the book of Proverbs. And meditate on the meaning of those proverbs. It will change your life. You can start, as I did years ago, with reading one chapter of Proverbs a day. It's easy to find the book of Proverbs. It's right in the middle of your Bible, next to Psalms. There are thirty-one chapters, so one a day works well. Each month, start over again. If you want to expand and read a psalm a day as well, that's good.

If you read the Bible, and take it to heart, for thirty or so years, you will be shocked at the blessing it will be to your life. I know I am.

WORDS THAT WILL
CHANGE YOUR LIFE

When I'm ranting and raving to my husband about some magazine that wouldn't buy my article or some person who was rude to me or someone who let me down, he says just four words to me. Four words that always make me angry—but are true. He says, "You have a choice." And even though I know what he means, I always say, "What?" and he repeats himself, "You have a choice. You can choose how you are going to respond to this." I hate that and I love it as well. We can choose. We can always choose how we will respond.

WORRY

I have a problem with worry. I worry so much that my husband calls me a Fret-o-saurus-rex (a dinosaur-sized worrier). I worry so much that if I were an evolutionist, I'd believe that one day all my worry would come together in a big bang and somehow explode into a something that actually did good in the world. Something that actually resolved problems.

But to date, all the worrying I've ever done over my husband and my daughter and the world at large hasn't changed one tiny circumstance, but it's changed me. It's made me more afraid and distrustful.

I'm thinking I'm going to give it up. After all, God tells us to give it up. He says don't worry about anything, pray about everything. And don't forget to be thankful.

My friend Connie says thanksgiving takes away worry. That when we are being thankful it's impossible to worry. I'm going to try that the next time worry hits me, like it's hitting me right now (What if no one likes this book? Auuggghhh!). I'm going to try the thankful thing: *Thank you, Lord, for the opportunity to write this book.* Yes, it does work. It does work.

If you are a worrier too, join me in the experiment of replacing our worry with prayers of thanksgiving. You've got nothing to lose except a headache. Your worry wasn't accomplishing any good anyway, even if you are an evolutionist.

You Will Always Be Ridiculed by Someone

Life is difficult. That's the way the author M. Scott Peck started his wonderful book *The Road Less Traveled*. Life is difficult. And that is how I want to end my little book.

If you accept this truth, it is easier to bear. Jesus said that in this world we will have tribulation. But somehow, we spend most of our lives in a rush to get away from tribulation.

I'd like to end on one more hard lesson, in addition to the truth about life being difficult. There will always be someone ridiculing you. It's just the way of life. No matter what your stance on any issue, it won't be popular with everyone. And if you don't take a stance, you will endure ridicule for that.

There are three responses to ridicule: (1) Ignore it, (2) diffuse it with humor, and (3) grow from it. I respond in all three ways on a daily basis.

ACKNOWLEDGMENTS

Besides my editor who was mentioned in the front of this manuscript, there are several people who contributed greatly to whatever good you may gain from this book:

Attorney Chris Ferebee of the law firm Yates & Yates. Being associated with the most feared and respected attorney in the industry gave me great confidence. Thank you, Chris Ferebee; thank you, Sealy Yates.

Connie Smiley, and her husband Don. While I was writing this book, I called Connie almost daily for her insight and wisdom. And for her great encouragement, I can never thank her enough.

Don Pape, my publisher, whom I used to be afraid of, but now whom I adore. Don, it is an honor to be published by the company you lead.

My husband, Tom, and my daughter, Mandy. If Tom didn't go to work each day to put a roof over my head and food in my mouth, and make money to buy my computer and pay my phone bills, and love me no matter what, this book would never have existed. And Mandy, I'm sure it was your prayers toward the end that helped me complete this book. "Dear Lord," you prayed, "*please* let my mommy finish her book." And so I have.

ABOUT THE AUTHOR

M arsha Marks is a popular speaker and author known for her ability to blend humor with spiritual insight. She is the author of *101 Amazing Things About God* and a former contributing editor to *Campus Life*. Her articles and stories have appeared in such publications as *Writer's Digest, Eternity, Moody Monthly,* and *The Christian Reader,* and she has appeared on numerous radio and television programs, including the Billy Graham Evangelistic Association's *Hour of Decision.* Her column, "A Few Minutes with Marsha," appears weekly in the *Effingham Herald.* Marsha and her family make their home in Savannah, Georgia.